Ethel L. Payne

The Power of Her Pen

To Marguerite Gonsalves—teacher, mentor, inspiration
—L. C-R.

To my uncles: Johnny, Martin, and James Matsko, with Michael H. and Joseph G.
—J. P.

SIMON & SCHUSTER BOOKS FOR YOUNG READERS
An imprint of Simon & Schuster Children's Publishing Division
1230 Avenue of the Americas, New York, New York 10020
Text copyright © 2020 by Lesa Cline-Ransome
Illustrations copyright © 2020 by John Parra
For information about special discounts for bulk purchases, please contact Simon & Schuster Special Sales
at 1-866-506-1949 or business@simonandschuster.com.
The Simon & Schuster Speakers Bureau can bring authors to your live event.
For more information or to book an event, contact the Simon & Schuster Speakers Bureau
at 1-866-248-3049 or visit our website at www.simonspeakers.com.
Book design by Laurent Linn
The text for this book was set in Egyptienne.
The illustrations for this book were rendered in acrylic paints on illustration board.
Photograph of Ethel L. Payne on p. 43 copyright © 2020 by Bettmann/GettyImages
Manufactured in China
0424 SCP
6 8 10 9 7
Library of Congress Cataloging-in-Publication Data
Names: Cline-Ransome, Lesa, author. | Parra, John, illustrator.
Title: The power of her pen : the story of groundbreaking journalist Ethel L. Payne / Lesa Cline-Ransome ;
illustrated by John Parra.
Description: First edition. | New York : Simon & Schuster Books for Young Readers, 2020.
| "A Paula Wiseman Book." | Includes bibliographical references.
Identifiers: LCCN 2019006401 | ISBN 9781481462891 (hardcover : alk. paper) | ISBN 9781481462907 (eBook)
Subjects: LCSH: Payne, Ethel L.—Juvenile literature. | Journalists—United States—Biography—Juvenile
literature. | African American women journalists—Biography—Juvenile literature.
Classification: LCC PN4874.P367 C55 2019 | DDC 070.92 [B]—dc23
LC record available at https://lccn.loc.gov/2019006401

The *Power* of Her Pen

The Story of Groundbreaking Journalist
Ethel L. Payne

WRITTEN BY
Lesa Cline-Ransome

ILLUSTRATED BY
John Parra

A Paula Wiseman Book
SIMON & SCHUSTER BOOKS FOR YOUNG READERS
New York London Toronto Sydney New Delhi

Ethel Lois Payne always had an ear for stories: her grandparents' front-porch stories of Kentucky cotton fields and Tennessee auction blocks. Her parents' kitchen-table stories of northbound trains from sharecroppers' plots. Long past her bedtime, Ethel collected the stories of people who followed a path paved with dreams.

In 1911, the year Ethel was born, her father, William, worked as a Pullman porter on railroad trains, helping passengers with their luggage and serving them in dining cars on trains that crisscrossed the country. He tossed bundles of a newspaper called the *Chicago Defender* onto train platforms, spreading news of jobs and hope for blacks in the segregated south. Ethel didn't see her daddy much, but his firm hand ruled from a distance. He and her mama, Bessie, a Latin teacher, filled their home with an equal measure of discipline and love.

On Saturdays, once the house was spotless, Bessie took Ethel and her five siblings to the white side of town, where there were libraries with shelves stacked tall with books. There, Ethel flipped through pages and memorized passages to recite to anyone who would listen.

One month after Ethel started high school, her father came home after a long run on the railroads and took to bed, sick with headache. The house was hushed, the doctor was called, but nothing could be done. After William passed, Bessie worked hard to make ends meet.

Ethel walked a mile to school each day. The neighborhood residents screamed and yelled and threw rocks at a black girl who dared to go to school with whites. "Sometimes I stood my ground, sometimes I got a bloody nose from fighting. But that was the way it was," Ethel later recalled.

Ethel spent her school days daydreaming of life far beyond her neighborhood—except when she was in English class. There, her teacher, Miss Dixon, encouraged her writing. Her mother encouraged her at home. Ethel wrote during the day, and she read her stories aloud to her family at night. The school wouldn't let a black student work on the school newspaper, but, after reading Ethel's writing, it did publish her very first story.

During the Great Depression, with money even tighter than before, Ethel attended a local college with free tuition and took writing classes.

When World War II began, the United States fought overseas while Ethel fought against racism and injustice in her own backyard. She started by organizing a women's social group at her church to make improvements in her community. Then she started a story hour for children. Next she started a scholarship fund.

After battling long and hard in Chicago, Ethel set her sights on politics in Washington, DC, and began writing letters to newspapers, commenting on unjust laws and discrimination against blacks. "I was beginning to have the seeds of rebellion churning up in me," Ethel later said.

By the time World War II ended in 1945, Ethel was aching to see a world far beyond the South Side of Chicago. She got the chance when she answered a newspaper ad for a job overseas. With her mother's blessing, she was on her way to Tokyo, Japan.

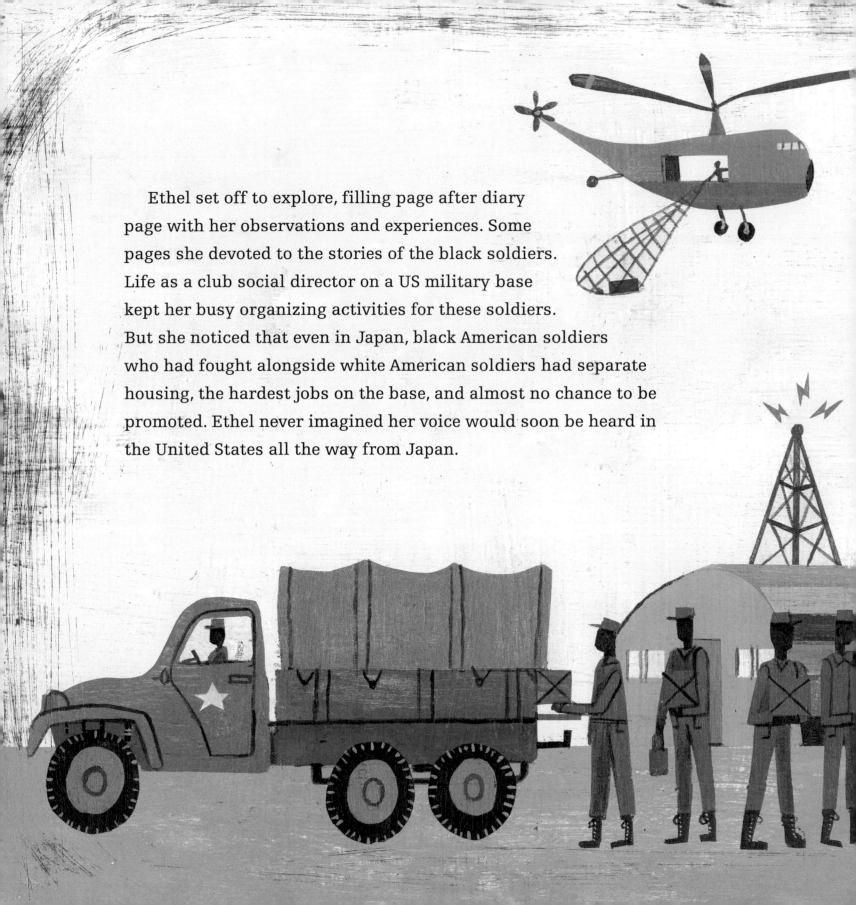

Ethel set off to explore, filling page after diary page with her observations and experiences. Some pages she devoted to the stories of the black soldiers. Life as a club social director on a US military base kept her busy organizing activities for these soldiers. But she noticed that even in Japan, black American soldiers who had fought alongside white American soldiers had separate housing, the hardest jobs on the base, and almost no chance to be promoted. Ethel never imagined her voice would soon be heard in the United States all the way from Japan.

Ethel showed her diary entries to a friend—a reporter who was on assignment in Japan. With Ethel's permission, he shared her writing with his editor back in Chicago.

Her sister was the first to call with the news. One of Ethel's articles about black soldiers stationed in Japan had made its way across the seas and into newspaper headlines, which were now in the hands of thousands.

When her job in Japan ended in 1951, Ethel
returned to her home, her family, and a job offer
from the *Chicago Defender*, one of the only two
daily black newspapers in the country and the
main source of news in the black community. It
celebrated the births, graduations, marriages, and
retirement news of its black citizens. Ethel once
joked, "You couldn't grow up in Chicago and be
black if you didn't know the *Chicago Defender*."

As the features reporter, Ethel wrote about housing, jobs, health care, and community events. After one year, Ethel and her notebook headed to the Democratic National Convention in Chicago, where politicians debated civil rights. As more and more readers opened their newspapers to read the articles written by Ethel L. Payne, the *Defender*'s circulation grew. After three years, her editor asked, "Why don't you go down to Washington?"

Of the two hundred and four reporters, Ethel was one of only three black journalists issued a White House press pass. It allowed her to sit in the Treaty Room of the White House, where the president met with journalists. Only when the president nodded could a reporter ask a question. These experienced reporters knew how to jump to their feet, hoping their voices would be the ones to reach the president's ears.

At first, Ethel sat waiting. Then she stood. Then she waited more. Finally, President Dwight D. Eisenhower turned to Ethel and nodded. "Mr. President . . . ," Ethel began shakily, "Mr. President . . ." She looked down at her carefully written question and asked the president's views on a racial incident that had occurred at the White House.

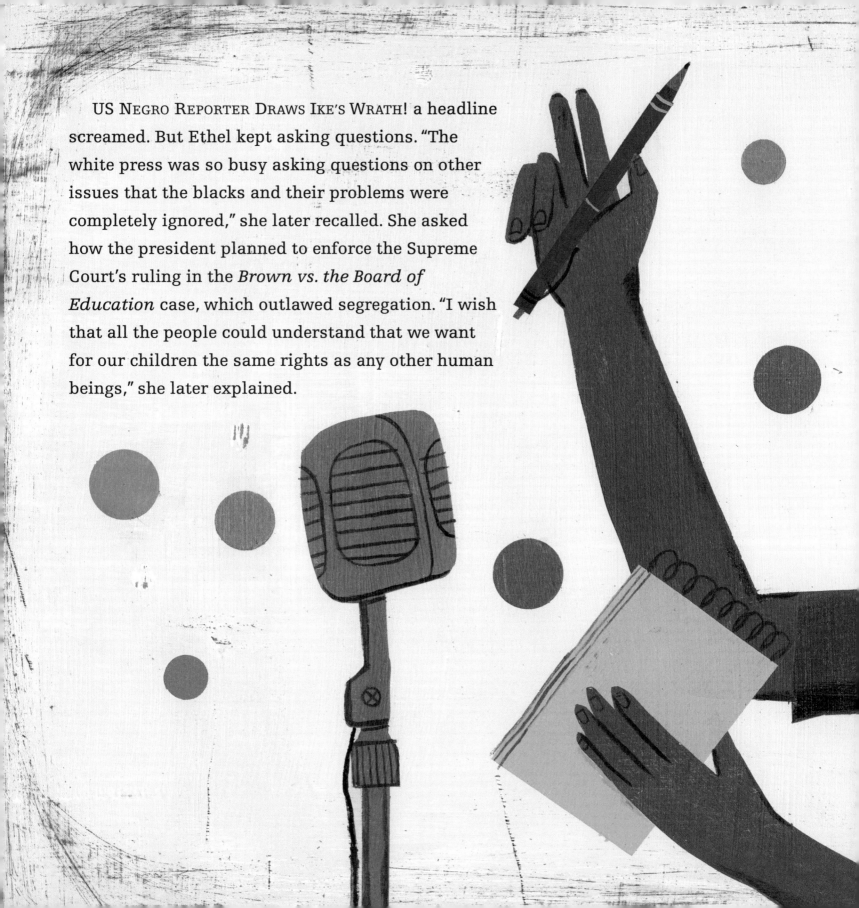

US NEGRO REPORTER DRAWS IKE'S WRATH! a headline screamed. But Ethel kept asking questions. "The white press was so busy asking questions on other issues that the blacks and their problems were completely ignored," she later recalled. She asked how the president planned to enforce the Supreme Court's ruling in the *Brown vs. the Board of Education* case, which outlawed segregation. "I wish that all the people could understand that we want for our children the same rights as any other human beings," she later explained.

1962

John F. Kennedy

VOTE

When Eisenhower left office in 1961, Ethel asked the young president John F. Kennedy about his civil rights voting record. When Kennedy was assassinated in 1963, she asked Lyndon B. Johnson about the Vietnam War and the Civil Rights Act. And then she asked Richard M. Nixon questions about the lack of blacks in his administration, and Jimmy Carter questions on education. Ethel spent so much time in the White House, she earned the title "First Lady of the Black Press."

1965

Lyndon B. Johnson

1969

Richard M. Nixon

1977

Jimmy Carter

Outside the White House, Ethel interviewed protesters in Montgomery, Alabama, and Little Rock, Arkansas, and marched alongside Dr. Martin Luther King Jr. across the Edmund Pettus Bridge in Selma, Alabama.

EDMUND PETTUS BRIDGE

"Somebody had to do the fighting, somebody had to speak up," Ethel later declared. Writing stories of the protesters' struggles was her way of doing just that.

For nearly five decades, Ethel fought long and hard to bring attention to the issues that mattered most to her community and became the voice of those who had none. Ethel wrote the stories that the mainstream media refused to. It was her questions to presidents that finally made readers of all races pay attention to the plight of African Americans.

Her reporting highlighted their struggle for justice, equal pay, housing, and education. And, in her role of informing her readers, Ethel created awareness and activism in the fight for civil rights for people across the globe.

Ethel L. Payne

Always with an ear for stories, Ethel asked the questions and demanded the answers for people whose paths were paved with dreams.

"I've had a box seat on history," Ethel once said, "and that's a rare thing."

AUTHOR'S NOTE

AS A YOUNG GIRL, I dreamed of becoming a hard-nosed reporter, sniffing out stories, uncovering cases of crime and corruption. But then, in high school, I attended a one-week workshop at a college in Boston, designed for students interested in entering the field of journalism. We met with local reporters and toured the floors of the *Boston Globe* newspaper. We created our own newspaper, for which I wrote several articles. But what I soon realized was that journalism would not be my chosen career. It takes a certain kind of grit and fearlessness I didn't yet possess at the age of seventeen.

Known as the "First Lady of the Black Press," Ethel Lois Payne possessed these qualities from the day she was born on August 14, 1911. Her passion for stories and truth and justice allowed her to be an ardent observer of the world and the people around her. When the mainstream, white press ignored stories of importance to the black community, Ethel used her pen and her voice to report on the Montgomery Bus boycott, Rosa Parks, the plight of unwed mothers, race relations, and the adoption crises for black children for the *Chicago Defender* newspaper, and she did so with authenticity and grace. Her pointed questions to numerous presidents elevated civil rights issues to the national agenda and, in turn, helped to speed along the slow wheels of change by holding elected officials accountable to their black constituents. In 1954, as one of the first African American White House press correspondents, she pushed President Dwight D. Eisenhower so hard for answers to her questions on desegregation, immigration, and anti-discrimination legislation, he stopped calling on her during press briefings. But it was her questions that prompted change in the form of Eisenhower's public stance and action on desegregation legislation.

Her reporting extended far beyond the United States. She traveled outside the country to report on African American soldiers serving in the Vietnam War, the Asian African Summit in Indonesia, the civil war in Nigeria, and apartheid in South Africa.

Upon her retirement from the press corps, President Lyndon B. Johnson presented her with the pens he used in the signing of the Civil and Voting Rights Acts.

As she aged, Ethel never slowed. She began teaching at the School of Journalism at Fisk University and became the first female African American commentator on a national television network.

Ethel Payne passed away on May 28, 1991, and left behind a legacy of speaking for the unheard and shining a light on injustice throughout the world. In 2002, she was one of four groundbreaking female journalists featured on a United States postage stamp.

"When it comes to issues that really affect my people . . . I think that I am an instrument of change."

—*Lesa Cline-Ransome*

SELECTED BIBLIOGRAPHY

Anderson, Ashlee. "Ethel Payne." The National Women's
    History Museum. July 31, 2018. womenshistory.org/
    education-resources/biographies/ethel-payne

Morris, James McGrath. *Eye on the Struggle: Ethel Payne, the
    First Lady of the Black Press*. New York: HarperCollins, 2015.

Morris, James McGrath, interview by Gwen Ifill, *PBS NewsHour*,
    PBS, February 26, 2015.

Viera, Bené. "If This Trailblazing Journalist Hadn't Been a Black
    Woman, You Would Know Her Name." timeline.com. March
    27, 2018.

SOURCE CREDITS

All quotations are from James McGrath Morris's *Eye on the
Struggle: Ethel Payne, the First Lady of the Black Press* (New
York: HarperCollins, 2015), with the exception of "When it
comes to issues . . . instrument of change," which is from James
McGrath Morris's "Ethel Payne, 'First Lady of the Black Press'
Asked Questions No One Else Would" (*Washington Post*,
August 12, 2011).

FURTHER READING

Atlas, Nava. *The Literary Ladies' Guide to the Writing Life: Inspiration and Advice from Celebrated Women Authors Who Paved the Way*. Portland, Maine: Sellers Publishing, Inc., 2011.

Harrison, Vashti. *Little Leaders: Bold Women in Black History*. New York: Little Brown Books for Young Readers, 2017.

Macy, Sue. *Miss Mary Reporting: The True Story of Sportswriter Mary Garber*. Illustrated by C. F. Payne. New York: Simon & Schuster Books for Young Readers, 2016.

Pinkney, Andrea Davis. *Let it Shine: Stories of Black Women Freedom Fighters*. Illustrated by Stephen Alcorn. New York: HMH Books for Young Readers, 2013.

Weatherford, Carole Boston. *Voice of Freedom: Fannie Lou Hamer: The Spirit of the Civil Rights Movement*. Illustrated by Ekua Holmes. Massachusetts: Candlewick Press, 2015.